·WALTER·CRANE'S·

·PICTURE·BOOKS·

·THE·

·ABSURD·

A·B·C

[ZHINGOORA BOOKS]

3

A for the APPLEor Alphabet pie,Which all get a slice of.Come taste it &
try.

B is the BABYwho gave Mr BuntingFull many a long day'srabbit skin
hunting.

C for the CATthat played on the fiddle,When cows jumped higher
than'Heigh Diddle Diddle!'

D for the DAMEwith her pig at the stile,'Tis said they got over,but not yet
a while.

E for the Englishman,
ready to make roar
The giant who wants to
have him for breakfast.

F for the Frog in the story
you know
Begun with a wooing but
ending in woe

G for Goosey Gander,
who wandered upstairs
And met the old man
who objected to prayers

E for the Englishman, ready to make fast The giant who wanted to have him for breakfast.

F for the Frog in the story you know, Begun with a wooing but ending in woe.

G for Goosey Ganderwho wandered upstairs,And met the old manwho objected to prayers.

H for poor Humpty who after his fall,
Felt obliged to resign his seat on the wall.

I for the Inn where they would fill your beer,
To one with too much and no more, I fear.

J does for poor Jack and also for Jill,
Who had so disastrous a tumble down hill.

H for poor Humpty whoafter his fall,Felt obliged to resign hisseat on the wall.

I for the Inn where theywouldn't give beer,To one with too muchand no money, I fear.

J does for poor Jack andalso for Jill,Who had so disastrousa tumble down hill.

K for calm Kitty, at dinnerwho sat,While all the good folkswatched the dog & the cat.

L for Little man, gun andbullets complete,Who shot the poor duck, andwas proud of the feat.

M for Miss Muffet, withthat horrid spider,Just dropped into tea anda chat beside her.

N for the Numerous childrenthey whoWere often too much fortheir mother in Shoe.

O the Old person thatcobwebs did spy,And went up to sweep 'emOh ever so high!

P for the Pie made of blackbirds to sing, A song fit for supper a dish for a king.

Q for Queen Anne
who sat in the sun
Till she, more than the lily
resembled the bun

R stands for Richard &
Robert, those men
Who didn't get up one
fine morning till ten!

S for the Snail that shows
wonderful fight,
Putting no less than twenty
four tailors to flight

Q for Queen Anne who sat in the sun Till she, more than the lily resembled the bun

R stands for Richard & Robert, those men Who didn't get up one fine morning till ten!

S for the Snail that showed wonderful fight, Putting no less than twenty-four tailors to flight!

T stands for Tom, the son of the piper, May his principles change as his years grow riper.

U for the Unicorn, keeping his eye on The coveted crown, and 'ts counsel the Lion.

V for the Victuals, including the drink, The old woman lived on surprising to think!

W for the WOMAN who not over nice, Made very short work of the three blind mice.

X is the X that is found upon buns, Which, daughters not liking, may come in for sons.

Y for Yankee Doodle of ancient renown, Both he & his pony that took him to town.

Z for the Zany wholooked like a fool, For when he was younghe neglected his school.

To   be   continue   soon....

The End